Colorad[...] History

Dona Herweck Rice

Table of Contents

Chapter 1

Colorado Long Ago

Colorado has been a state for a long time. But it has a history far older than its statehood.

To explore the history of Colorado, we need to look back in time thousands of years. Back before anyone in U.S. history can remember. Back before people wrote down what they did for future people to read.

In this time long ago, the towering mountains we now know as the Rockies were strung across the land. Wide plains spread out east of the mountains. The Grand Mesa stretched its wide, flat top into the western clouds. But no buildings sprouted from the landscape. No highways crossed the plains. And the night sky, free from city lights, was lit with more stars than the eye could see.

Grand Mesa

Grand Mesa is the largest mesa, or flat-topped mountain, in the world. Volcanoes formed it 10 million years ago. Over time, **erosion** has molded it to what we see today.

Pueblo Peoples

The first humans came to the area we know as Colorado about 14,000 years ago. They were **nomads**, following **game** for food. As time went on and they learned new skills, they started to put down roots. The people learned to grow plants for food. They hunted small, local game. They also became experts at making baskets, weaving, and pottery. Using **adobe**, wood, and stone, they built dwellings that would last. In fact, some of those dwellings still exist!

Puebloan pottery

Much of the land was **arid** even then, so storing water was key. They learned to build reservoirs and dams, much as people do now. By doing this, water was there when they needed it. They lived like this for a very long time. Today, we know them as the Pueblo peoples.

Cliff Palace

This city built of stone was made by the Pueblo peoples long ago. Today, it is a part of Mesa Verde National Park.

American Indians

The Pueblo peoples were attracted by the rich **natural resources** found here. There was plenty of all they needed for a good life. They had ample food and access to water. The land was good for growing maize, squash, and beans. The Pueblo peoples learned to thrive in the climate.

In time, others came to this place as well. The Ute Indian Tribe lived in the state by the 1600s. They settled mainly in the mountains and west. Some of the peoples moved with the seasons and to hunt.

The Ute peoples would one day become excellent horse riders. They first got horses from Spanish settlers. They used the horses for travel and during war. But they also had contests, such as horse races, to show their riding skills. Their skills with horses became a source of great pride among the Ute peoples.

a group of Ute horse riders

An American Indian man hunts bison.

Stewards of the Earth

The Ute peoples alternated hunting and gathering crops. They also moved from place to place over time. They did this to care for the land and allow it to replenish.

Maize was a common crop for the Ute peoples.

The peoples of the Apache Nation were the next to come. They settled in the plains of the East. They were **hunter-gatherers**. Some gathered food that grew from the ground. Others hunted bison and small game across the plains.

The peoples of the Comanche Nation came in the early 1700s. With the Utes, they forced the Apache peoples south. The Comanche peoples were also eventually pushed south. The Arapaho and Cheyenne Nations took over their land.

The various nations traded with each other. Pots and baskets might be traded for shells and beads. Crops might be traded for horses. Sometimes the nations fought. Even so, they all thrived in Colorado for many years.

Colorful

The Spanish word *colorado* means "red" and also "colorful." Early Spanish explorers noticed the red rocks and soil. They named the area after its colors.

members of the Comanche Nation

Roxborough State Park

Conquistadors

In the 1500s, people from Europe came to explore the land. The first to arrive were conquistadors from Spain. They came to explore and to conquer. They claimed the land for their own.

In 1706, Spain claimed Colorado as a province. This means it belonged to Spain. At least, it belonged to Spain as far as Spain was concerned. But those already living here did not see it this way.

The people from Spain began to trade with the native peoples. They started settlements as well. Soon enough, other settlers from Europe arrived. They claimed their own rights to the land. None of these groups acknowledged that the land was already home to those who had lived here for centuries.

Conquistadors

This word comes from the Spanish word *conquistadores*. It means "conquerors." The role of the conquistadors was to conquer and claim land for their homeland.

Chapter 2

Colorado in the 1800s

At the start of the new century, the United States was eager to expand. People felt crowded. They wanted land to farm and call their own. They needed resources to build the growing nation.

Thomas Jefferson was president. In 1803, he made a deal with France to buy a large section of land. This was called the Louisiana Purchase. The land reached north to Canada and west to the Rocky Mountains. It doubled the size of the nation.

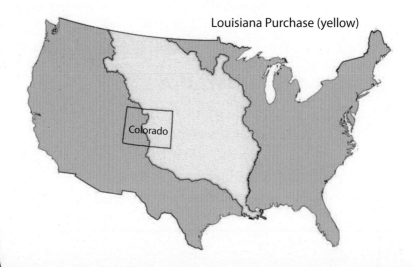

Louisiana Purchase (yellow)

Colorado

Pikes Peak

Pikes Peak is one of the most famous mountains in Colorado. It was called *Tava*, or "sun mountain," by the Ute peoples. Pike called it "Highest Peak." Later, others added his name and called it "Pike's Highest Peak." Now, it is simply Pikes Peak.

But there was a problem. Spain claimed rule over some of this land. In 1806, the U.S. Army sent an exploration group into this area. The group was led by Zebulon Pike. They wanted details about the land. And they wanted to know about its resources. The Pike party learned a lot. But they were arrested by Spanish soldiers. The group was sent to Mexico and later released.

Zebulon Pike

The next years were filled with struggles among the United States, Mexico, and Spain. Each wanted the same land. All the while, native peoples called the land their home.

Mexico won its freedom from Spain in 1821. It claimed some of Spain's **territories**. More and more trappers and traders moved to this area. They set up trading posts, mainly along rivers. The water made it easy to **transport** goods. Bent's Fort became a key outpost. It still stands. American Indians sometimes traded there.

But the United States still wanted to claim the land. It was eager to expand west. So, the United States and Mexico went to war. In the end, Mexico gave up some of its lands in the north. The treaty they made opened Colorado to settlers.

Bent's Fort

This map highlights the Spanish territories.

Treaties

The Treaty of Guadalupe-Hidalgo
(right) was signed in 1848. Land that
is now Arizona, California, Colorado,
Nevada, New Mexico, Texas, and
Utah became part of the United
States. The people living there
became U.S. citizens. In 1849,
another treaty was signed with the
Ute Nation. It opened Colorado to
U.S. settlement.

Colorado Gold Rush

Expansion into Colorado took off in one big rush. A gold rush, to be exact. The Colorado gold rush was set in motion when a **wagon train** crossed the South Platte River at Clear Creek. Lewis Ralston dipped his gold pan into the water. He came up with about five dollars in gold.

The wagon train moved on. But eight years later, in 1858, Ralston returned with the William Green Russell party. Rumors of the gold they found quickly made their way east. In short order, about 100,000 people flooded to Colorado, searching for gold. The gold in the water soon ran out. So, miners took to the mountains. They searched for seams of gold and other minerals there. Some struck it rich. Most just labored. But **boom towns** sprouted up all over.

Barney Ford

Barney Ford had been enslaved but came to Colorado seeking his fortune. Because he was Black, he was not allowed to mine. But he started several businesses, such as hotels and restaurants. He made a fortune and became one of the richest people in Colorado.

Centennial State

As the population grew, so did the belief that Colorado should become a state. In 1859, it became part of two U.S. territories. Two years later, it was redrawn as the Territory of Colorado. It belonged to the United States. Since it did, the country could use its resources. The Union did just that during the Civil War.

Attempts were made to make it a state. But there were blocks. Some people did not want to pay state taxes. Others thought miners would not be good citizens. Many people wanted to give Black people the right to vote. But some people did not want this. A group wanted the two senators allowed for a state to be added to the U.S. Congress. Others feared that any new senators would not agree with their **party**. Statehood was argued for years.

World's Sanatorium

Colorado's climate was thought to be healthy, especially for people with lung diseases, such as tuberculosis. In the 1860s, many came here to get healthy. Colorado became known as the "world's **sanatorium**."

Doc Holliday, a famous figure in the Old West, came to Colorado for his health.

In the end, it came down to the railroads. Colorado did not have many. People there could not travel with ease by train. The people of Denver wanted to change this. They pooled their money to help build the Denver Pacific Railroad. It linked Denver with points north. Then, the Kansas Pacific Railroad was complete. It linked towns from Denver through Kansas.

The trains helped Denver become a major city in the West. This helped ensure statehood. On August 1, 1876, President Ulysses S. Grant signed the order. It made Colorado a state. This was just days after the country's 100-year birthday. They called it the **Centennial** State.

Railways were important in Denver, the capital city since 1867.

Casimiro Barela

Barela became a well-known lawmaker in Colorado. Born in Mexico, he helped Mexicans who had just become U.S. citizens keep their lands and be treated fairly. He also made sure that the state constitution was written in a few languages. In this way, many groups of people living in the state could read it.

The Battle Goes On

But statehood did not bring peace. The state was home to many American Indians. They did not want to go just because settlers were taking the land. In 1864, U.S. soldiers killed 150 peaceful native people. The native people thought they were protected by the law. Instead, they were **massacred**. This event is known today as the Sand Creek Massacre.

A two-year war followed. It was fought mainly between settlers and native peoples. Four Indian nations joined forces. They tried to keep their lands and way of life. In the end, many were killed or cast out of the state.

Some fighting went on through the 1880s. It stopped at the end of the decade. By then, most Indian nations were overrun and forced to move. The Ute peoples remained in Colorado on a large reservation.

The Ute Treaty of 1868

This treaty was struck between the U.S. government and leaders of the Ute Indian Tribe. The Ute peoples agreed to give up their claim to the central Rockies. In exchange, they accepted a large reservation in the southwest region of the state.

Chapter 3

Colorado Today

Colorado's population grew once it became a state. The railroads made it easier for people to get there. The end of the fighting with the native peoples appealed to new settlers too. Many felt a pull to travel to the West. In 1893, the state also gave women the right to vote. Only Wyoming had done this so far.

Industries began to flourish. Mining remained a key business. Other industries grew as well. **Manufacturing** plants sprouted up. They made goods such as steel, rubber, and cotton cloth. Some people canned foods. Others made airplanes. Farming continued to be a major business in the state. Livestock was raised and sold too.

In the 1930s, a new industry took hold. People found that the Rockies were a great place to ski. Skiing has been big business ever since.

Much of Colorado's natural beauty remains today.

"America, the Beautiful"

This famous song was written by Katherine Lee Bates (shown above). She wrote it after a climb to the top of Pikes Peak in 1893. Colorado has long been known for its beauty.

As the century wore on, new industries came to be. The Great Depression and the two World Wars caused **economic** hardships. This was true around the world. But new businesses rose from them as well. Mid-century, people in the state mined and made parts for nuclear weapons. Then, as the computer industry grew, Colorado took part. Today, it is known as a tech hub. Some major tech companies make their home in the state.

Colorado has also become a leader in clean energy. Such energy can be renewed. It does not harm the environment. Solar and wind energy are widely used here.

Tourism has remained one of the key industries in the state. The beauty of nature draws people from around the world. They come year-round to see the sites and play.

Rocky Flats Plant, a plutonium recovery facility

Hikers explore the Rockies.

No Games

Colorado is the only state to turn down hosting the Olympics. The people of the state voted *no* to paying the taxes it would take. The 1976 Winter Olympic Games were moved to Austria instead.

Cityscapes

Through the last century, major cities took shape. Denver was made the capital even before statehood. It is a transportation hub. Its airport is one of the busiest in the nation and even the world. Cars and trains buzz through Denver around the clock. There are many office centers and colleges in and around the city. It is a center for culture too.

Colorado Springs has been a major tourist spot for many decades. Boulder is known for its college life, art, and culture. Both became cities about the same time Colorado was made a state. Grand Junction is known for its fruit and wine. Aspen, Telluride, and Vail are all well-known for their sport. The first two date back to the early days of statehood. Vail is much newer. It was formed in the 1960s.

Denver International Airport

1966 Broncos

Good Sports

Denver hosts many professional sports teams. The Denver Broncos, its football team, was formed in 1961.

Moving Forward

Colorado's history goes back a very long time. But it is also a place known for moving forward. It is a leader when it comes to new forms of energy and technology. It is at the forefront in matters of social justice and equal rights. It paves the way when it comes to caring for the land, water, and air. It tries to protect people and places now so they have a bright future ahead.

Ute children today learn the language.

The Ute Indian Tribe is the oldest group of peoples in the state. They have a strong community and culture even now. But Colorado is also home to diverse groups of people from many cultures. It takes pride in its diversity. And it welcomes all who would like to call Colorado their home.

Tall Facts

Colorado has the highest elevation of all the states. The city of Leadville has the highest elevation of all U.S. cities. The state has the highest railway, the highest auto tunnel, and the highest suspension bridge in the world.

Coloradans march for a social justice cause.

Chapter 4

Chin Lin Sou: "Mayor of Chinatown"

Chin Lin Sou was born in China. He became a leader in Colorado.

When Chin was a young man, he heard about jobs in America. He left his family to work on the Transcontinental Railroad. The railroad was meant to connect the American East and West. Many Chinese men were hired to do this back-breaking work. Chin spoke fluent English and Chinese. He was also more than 6 feet (nearly 2 meters) tall. His height and English fluency earned him the job of railroad overseer.

When the railroad was finished, the workers lost their jobs. Many tried mining. This was also hard work and did not earn much for most miners. But Chin became a supervisor again and made a good living. After 10 years apart, he was able to bring his wife from China. They had a family. Then, Chin found and sold two gold mines. They were rich!

a stained-glass image of Chin (top)

Transcontinental Railroad

This great stretch of railway took six years to build. It was done mainly by hand. The work was very dangerous. Workers drove spikes into mountain rock. They filled the holes with black powder and set off explosions to clear the way. Many workers were badly injured or killed.

Riots against Chinese immigrants became common.

Chin and his family moved to Denver. There was much anti-Chinese feeling at the time. Many people did not welcome the immigrants. Some were violent. Chin tried to protect the Chinese people and help them get jobs. He became a leader among them.

Chin opened a trading company in Denver. He **imported** goods from China. These were things such as food and clothing. He became a big success. Some called Chin the "Mayor of Chinatown." He was an inspiration to them.

In 1894, Chin became ill and died. But his **legacy** lives on. Many of his **descendants** still live in the area. A stained-glass window was placed in the Colorado State capitol building. It is a picture of Chin for all to see and remember.

Congress of the United States, At the First Session,

Begun and held at the CITY OF WASHINGTON, in the DISTRICT OF COLUMBIA, on Monday, the fifth day of December, eighteen hundred and eighty-

An Act

To execute certain treaty stipulations relating to Chinese

Whereas, In the opinion of the Government of the United States the coming of Chinese laborers to this country endangers the good order of certain localities within the territory thereof: Therefore, Be it enacted by the Senate and House of Representatives of the United States of America in Congress assembled, That from and after the expiration of ninety days next after the passage of this act, and until the expiration of ten years next after the passage of this act, the coming of Chinese laborers to the United States be, and the same is hereby, suspended; and during such suspension it shall not be lawful for any Chinese laborer to come, or, having so come after the expiration of said ninety days, to remain within the United States.

SEC. 2. That the master of any vessel who shall knowingly bring within the United States on such vessel, and land or permit to be landed, any Chinese laborer ...

Chinese Exclusion Act

Some people in the United States said that immigrants from China were taking their jobs. Some of them became violent toward the immigrants. The government passed the Chinese Exclusion Act in 1882. This kept most Chinese people from becoming citizens. The act was in effect until 1943.

37

Glossary

arid—dry

adobe—a type of brick made of mud and straw and baked dry in the sun

boom towns—communities that sprout up quickly, often because of a money-making opportunity

centennial—100-year anniversary

descendants—people who are related to a person or group of people from the past

economic—having to do with money

erosion—the wearing of rock and soil through the natural movement of water and wind

game—animals that are hunted for food

hunter-gatherers—groups of people who get food by gathering plants and hunting wildlife

imported—brought from another country to be sold

legacy—something that comes from someone in the past, often something good

manufacturing—the business of making products, especially with machines

massacred—killed brutally and intentionally

natural resources—materials that come from nature and can be used to make money

nomads—people who move from place to place, usually due to weather and resources

party—a political group that shares the same ideas and values and nominates candidates for office

sanatorium—a medical facility for those suffering from a long-term illness

territories—areas of land that belong to a government and have its protection but limited rights

transport—move from one place to another

wagon train—a group of covered wagons traveling together across a long distance for safety and support

Index

History in Your Community

Colorado has a long and rich history. It has changed a lot over the years. Your community has a history, too, and it is also changing. What do you know about the history where you live? You can research the history of your community. Here are some things to do:

1. Look online.

2. Visit your city hall or chamber of commerce.

3. Talk with a librarian at your community library. Read old community newspapers there.

4. Talk with the adults in your life who have lived in your community a long time.

5. Make a timeline of your community's history with photos and drawings. Share it with your family to teach them about the history where you live.